# Gemstones

By Heather Hammonds

## Contents

# How Gemstones Are Mined

Gemstones are minerals found in the earth.

Most gemstones are dug from the ground, at mines.

Gemstones are cut and polished into gems.

There are many different gems,
such as diamonds, rubies and emeralds.

Miners dig tunnels deep underground
in places where gemstones are found.

Rock and earth are brought to the surface
of the mine. The gemstones are then removed
from the rock and earth.

Some mines are cut into the top of the land.

Miners dig gigantic holes in the land
so they can find gemstones in the rock and earth.

Some mines are very large.
Many gemstones are found at these mines.

Hundreds of people work at large mines.
Mine workers live in towns, by the mines.

Small mines may be owned by one or two miners.

The miners work in their own mine.
They dig the rock, earth and gemstones
from the mine without the help of other miners.

Gemstones such as diamonds cost a lot of money because they are hard to find.

Gemstones such as quartz do not cost as much money as diamonds because they are easier to find.

uncut gemstones

Gemstones usually cost more after they have been cut and polished into gems.

**cut and polished gems**

# Working at a Diamond Mine

My dad works at a diamond mine.
One day, I would like to work in a mine, too.

I think a diamond mine is a very exciting place to work.

First, there are many different jobs at the mine where Dad works.
You can drive a giant truck,
or dig for diamonds in very deep mines under the ground.

Second, the mine where Dad works is far away from cities and towns.
People fly in aeroplanes to work at the mine.
It would be fun to fly to work in an aeroplane.

Third, people live and work at the mine
for two weeks at a time.
Then they have two weeks' holiday.
This means they can fly home
to visit family and friends.

| Joe Bowden | |
| --- | --- |
| Week 1 | working |
| Week 2 | working |
| Week 3 | leave |
| Week 4 | leave |

Joe Bowden works two weeks in every four

Fourth, it is safe to work at the mine. There are many safety rules that miners have to follow so they don't get hurt.

Doctors work at the mine to help anyone who becomes sick.

Last, there are sports buildings, a running track and shops at the mine.

Miners go shopping and play sport when they are not working.

I think mining for diamonds is a very good job.
Diamond miners help find
some of the most beautiful gemstones in the world!